The Hopeless Cooks Cook Book

By the same Author:
Profitable Hobbies & How to Market Them
Take Me Back to the Eighties (Text Only)

The Hopeless Cooks Cook Book

by
Carol Staines

Pinedale Press

Published by Pinedale Press,
   2 Lethbridge Ct.,
   Caloundra. 4551 Qld.
   Australia.
Illustrated by: Tina Homer

Copyright © 1985 Carol Staines
All rights reserved
Apart from private study, research or review as permitted under the Copyright Act, no part by means of any process should be reproduced without written permission.

First Published April 1986
Second Printing Sept 1986
Third Printing Sept 1989

National Library of Australia Cataloguing
in Publication Data
Staines Carol, 1945
ISBN 0   9593024   5   X

All names in this book are entirely ficticious

Contents

Hints N Tips   8

Meals With Meat   29

Meals Without Meat   51

Sweetmeats 70

Desserts 76

Miscellaneous 86

Dear Hopeless Cook,

Cooking really is a bore which is a pity when eating is such fun. The purpose of this book is not to make you feel guilty about the amount of time you do or don't spend in the kitchen.
Nor is it to show you magnificent photographs of food that make you drool at the mouth even though they are so complicated you'd never get around to making them. However, like most things in life, cooking just has to be done – by someone – usually yourself I guess.
This book will, I hope, keep you in the frying pan and out of the fire. I want to show you how to actually SURVIVE the cooking crisis, give you some foolproof recipies to cut down time in the kitchen and also to put a little more fun into it.
By the way, the large print isn't because you need spectacles. Rather it is to make life easier when poised between such feats as cracking an egg INTO a bowl and reading what's to come next in the recipe.
So, best of everything, including the kitchen sink!

Hints N Tips to Make Life Easier in the Kitchen

As if cooking wasn't enough, there is always the washing up, menu planning and other boring jobs that demand attention from the cook.
Hints N Tips should make life easier and help cope with those nasties that seem to plague anyone who has to spend time in the kitchen.

Index

Ways to Escape from Cooking & Washing Up
How to Soothe Frayed Nerves after Supercook Calls
Getting Your Own Back
What to Do If ...
A Little of Everything & Not Much of Anything
Why Cook Every Night?
Coping with Unexpected Company
Behind Schedule & Meal Time Looming Up
Effortless Ways to Brighten Kitchen China & Cutlery
Meeting Social Obligations Without too Much Fuss
Plain Sailing in the Kitchen
Making the Most of Kitchen Slaves
To Serve with Flair

Ways to Escape from Cooking & Washing Up

Major on Presentation

Even in the most Exclusive Establishments, raw food (yes raw) is consumed and considered a great treat. The trick is convince your hungry horde that really it is the 'art of fine food'. The fact that it saves pots and pans is just a side issue and really not even worth mentioning.

Here are some tips on how to do it:-

- Serve small portions only with a garnish, particularly as it is a new concept.

- A well presented salad is quicker and easier than cooking. This needn't necessarily mean sixteen or so different salad items. Rather it means think a little more on how it could look on the plate.

- Many children often prefer raw vegetables. By arranging these and fruits around a dip and letting diners 'choose and dip' it actually looks like a treat.

Lunch in a Basket

Now this really saves the washing up and looks special. Lay some paper serviettes or paper kitchen towelling in a cane basket and serve sandwiches, a slice of cake etc and a piece of fruit together. Everyone has their own basket. After the meal, dispose of the paper and store the baskets.

Fish N Chip Shop Trick

If the fish and chip shop can serve it up in paper, so can you. Make it a little more 'meant' by wrapping everyone's serving individually. After the meal, throw all the papers in the bin and hang up the teatowel.

Veges – Skins and All

Nutritionists tell us we should eat vegetable skins. How kind of them. In fact, it is a good way out for not peeling them. If anyone dares prod the veges and say they are not peeled, simply smirk and tell them you have their nutritional interests at heart.

Cook or Steam Vegetables Together

Carrots and peas look appealing as the bright colours glow together. Any other combination that takes your fancy can be made as well. If steamed, the vitamin content of the food is greater. Its a matter that 'all in together' means less pots in the sink.

Use Aluminium Foil

Line with aluminium foil every cooking dish you can to save mess and washing up. If money is an objection, then soothe your mind because foil is cheaper then handcream.

Oven to Table Ware

Use Oven to Table ware as much as possible to save dirtying too many items. Its mainly a matter of getting into the habit of doing this. A few conscious efforts on your part and then it will become second nature. Dishes that have at least two compartments are the cook's dream.

How to Soothe Frayed Nerves After Supercook Calls

Read this page only after your nerves are frayed and Supercook has departed. I hope it will make you feel better.

1. A full larder and an overflowing cookie barrel are not indicative of a mother's love to her family. (Conversely, neither is an empty one.)
2. Over provided children do not always adjust well in adult life. They find it harder to manage.
3. Everyone keeps thinner and trimmer without a la carte meals.
4. Cooking is not the sole perogative of one person per household. After all, the cook may feel like a sickie occasionally. There really is no point feeling guilty.
5. Its not your problem you were born a non cook. After all, its not fair to shine in all areas.
6. Oh no ... the clock says the hungry tribe will be wanting something to eat soon. Well, why not let your friend the takeaway shop help you out .... just this once?

Getting Your Own Back

Has anyone ever told you how wonderful it is to be a homemaker and smugly raved on about their latest culinary feat when they know full well that it is in other areas you excel and definitely not cooking!

Here is a chance to bite your tongue and smile sweetly and wait for the opportune moment to come. Simply tell them you have to run because tonight you intend cooking "Saucisse et Pomme de Terre (pronounced So-siss a pom-de-ter) for dinner and preparations just have to start about now.

By the way, it really is a fancified name for Bangers and Mash but that is your secret (unless they know French as well.)

Here then, is the culinary masterpiece guide for you to follow.

Saucisse et Pomme de Terre
(Alias Bangers and Mash)

Simmer sausages in water for about 10 minutes till cooked.
Remove skins.
Put sausages in a frying pan on medium heat to brown.
Boil potatoes till cooked. (that is the pom de terre part)
Serve before the delicious smell from the kitchen forces the hungry horde to attack and lay seige on the kitchen.
P.S. If you have ever wondered why sausages have fat in them ... well its to do with the flavour they say.

Trouble Shooting

Its all going fine and then it is suddenly discovered there are no spuds, greens, eggs or whatever and your happy world then turns a nasty shade of blue.

Cheer up, here are some ways around this dilemma:

If you Need	Try Using These Substitutes
An egg	1 Tab powdered milk for each egg
	1 Tab golden syrup for each egg
Spuds	Macaroni, rice
	None of those – extra vege. After all, there is no law that says you must eat spuds.
Sugar	Honey, golden syrup (use less quantity as sweeter than sugar) jam.

Thickener for gravy etc	Use sago – cook 15 minutes longer till clear rolled oats breadcrumbs
More veges	If low on veges, make one layered dish with left behinds. This will make one acceptable sized item which doesn't look like only one carrot, one spud etc. Grease an ovenware dish Parboil veges Layer till all used Moisten with about 1 cup milk/water Put in about 180 degrees oven for about 45-60 minutes till cooked

What to Do If ...

You may have opened the cupboard like Old Mother Hubbard and found it nearly bare, except for maybe, a hunk of cheese, a few veges or an egg or so.

After the initial shock of the state of affairs, assemble all the items that could be used on the table.

This really is a helpful ploy to sort out WHAT to cook.

The list below may help solve the problem and put a meal on the table for you. In fact, you may be pleasantly surprised at the results.

Left in Cupboards	What to Cook
Spuds	Potato Fritters Potato Casserole
Cheese	Pizza Cheese Pie Hasty N Tasty Easy Bake

Eggs	Savoury/Sweet Pancakes
	Cheese Pie
	Eggs in Curry
Tin of Fish	Fish Pie
	Fish Mornay
Vegetables Only	Vegetable Lunch Dish
	Savoury Pancakes

A Little of Everything and Not Much of Anything

This situation can turn a normal human being into a despairing lump of jelly. Sure, there is plenty in the Fridge but not enough to make a decent meal of any one thing.

Here is a solution that is EASY, LOOKS GREAT, and more important, SOLVES THE PROBLEM.

Take out what is left in the Fridge and sort out what could be used. Look in the vegie bin and even the fruit bowl. This will be Kebab Time.

Kebabs

Simply thread on to a skewer for each person and brown under the griller.

It could look like this:
    Left over sausage/chicken/meat
    Tomato – cubed
    Piece boiled spud
    Pineapple piece, apple, peach apricot (tinned or fresh)
    Thread on and repeat until skewer is full.

If there are any noodles/macaroni/rice around, this will be ideal to cook to lay the kebabs on and of course eat with it. If not, a lettuce leaf or any salad items will do the trick for you.

Why Cook Every Night?

There is no rule that says "Thou shalt always do the cooking – every night, every meal". Naturalists are always warning us not to continuously feed the wildlife because they will become dependent on us and really, they will starve if for some reason the feeding stops. To help the family mature and grow into healthy adults or keep them that way if they already are it is not in their interests to do all the cooking.

After all, if Tom Sawyer could teach his friends that painting the fence was really a privilege, then maybe it could work for you when it comes to cooking. Why not bow out occasionally and give them a try.

It may be a shock for the first time but when they see it is 'cook or starve', I think you may be pleasantly surprised.

It may help to have a simple recipe in mind in case the excuse is given they wouldn't know what to cook. To help you out, turn to page no 62 "Cooks Night off Special" and leave it open. I don't think anyone could come to harm making it seeing it is just so simple. Warning – Praise their efforts.

After all, its better for them to be standing at the kitchen sink than having to do it yourself.

Double Up and Freeze

Not you, of course, but whatever is being cooked. It only takes a little more effort to make a double quantity and freeze a portion of it.

Console yourself by thinking how marvelous it will be when one night all that has to be done is take the extra portion out of the freezer and pop it in the oven after it has thawed.

It really is worth the effort and once in the habit of it, you'll wonder why the little old brain didn't advise you to try this trick before.

Unexpected Company

Why is it that 10 minutes before meal time someone suddenly remembers that Harry, Fred, Mary or Jane (or worse still, all of them) have been invited for dinner. As a rule, this person is generally 6 foot tall and eats like a horse.

Here are some tricks to help you out of this predicament besides going berserk with a meataxe. If you did, go berserk with a meataxe I mean, I guess no one would stay around long enough to see what was for dinner anyhow!

Add more Spuds

If there aren't a lot, serve them in chunks. The chewing will fill up the corners easier than if they are mashed and 'slide down'.

Add more Gravy

Put more water or milk in and thicken with flour/gravy make or throw in some breadcrumbs especially if mince etc.

Pastry/Breads are Filling

Butter some bread, place on top of whatever and pop under the griller to form a crust or a 'pastry lid'.

Mince Stretcher

If mince is on the menu, make it a meat sauce instead. This really is a runny mince and poured over spaghetti, rice or potatoes is good news in the meal stretching department. Curry if you wish.

Use Smaller Plates

This makes the meal look bigger. Nothing is more depressing than a large plate with a meagre portion on it.

Serve Pre Dinner Nibbles

Sit everyone down to make it look like the gracious dining ritual performed at your address. Serve a drink with cheese crackers, diced raw veges and a dip (sauce and grated cheese if stuck).
This should, with the drink (even a cup of tea), take the edge off the appetites.

Serve soup as a first course, if you can

Being a liquid and especially if enriched with milk (fresh, powdered, cream), it will really round the corners off large appetites.
Grated cheese on top makes it still more filling. A pile of toast smells so good it will soon disappear. Cut into fingers or triangles and it will look as this was how things were intended.
Note – The larger the pile of toast, the more is eaten. After all, its better to have lots if the second course is going to be a little light on.
Ever noticed how some people seem to eat if they had hollow legs whilst others only nibble at their food. Now wouldn't it be a shame if you served up the nibbler far too much and the 'hungry horse' not enough. To overcome this problem, put all food on the table in dishes and let the diners select their own amount. I realize you may feel you'll have heart failure but in reality it seems to work out quite well.
No food is wasted and if there is anything left in the dishes, 'hungry horse' will soon remedy the situation.

Behind Schedule & Meal Time Looming Up

When there are gentle reminders given that meal time should not be too far away, get your own back by fooling everyone that preparations are underway and food will appear sometime in the not too distant future.

Set the Table

Everyone seems to think that if the table is set, it stands to reason that food will follow shortly.

Produce an Aroma

Fry some onions, the smell will satisfy everyone and if they pester you, give them some to pick at. After all, isn't it better to pick at some onions than for them to pick at you!

Keep Them Occupied

Make a cup of tea/coffee for everyone so they can relax before eating. There is just so much scientific data that warns to be careful about eating in a rushed state. It also creates an atmosphere of being loved and cosseted. The fact it gives you a further 15-20 minutes for food preparation is rather immaterial!

Effortless Ways to Clean China

This is NOT recommended for Royal Doulton or Royal Anything but is simply great for everyday cups and saucers.

It generally happens that visitors come at reasonably short notice. It also generally happens that the cups and saucers have stains on them which look odiously obvious.
Here is a simple solution:
> Fill the sink with water
> Add about 1 cupful of household bleach
> Carefully load the cups, saucers etc into the sink
> Leave soak until stains gone (about 10 minutes)
> Wash in hot water to remove smell
> If you use very hot water, they automatically dry.
> Can be used immediately.

To Brighten Up Cutlery

Add some laundry detergent
Stand cutlery in jug for about 10 minutes
Wash well
Use

Needless to say, it is not the treatment for fine silverware, just the ordinary everyday sort.

Fullfilling Social Obligations Without Much Sweat

Its now your turn to have the gang around or there is a special function looming up on the horizon. The mere thought of 12 or so hungry bodies coming in the door does wonders for the morale! Before you end up a jibbering heap, here is an easy plan to make life a little easier.

Forget about a sit down dinner. It can be, as you are probably very much aware, a lot of work serving up 12 plates. Besides it is quite possible there isn't enough bench space to attempt such a feat.
The easiest way out is to make the guests do the work for you in an unsuspecting manner. The term used to perform such a trick is called 'smorgasbord'

In reality, everyone does a little share of the work by serving themselves. It also means that cold dishes can be laid out prior to the folk arriving and the hot ones can be kept in the oven. This really simplifies matters. All that has to be done at the last moment is to take the hot dishes from the oven and place on the table. There is no worry about dribbling the gravy and if the vegetables are growing cold. Another side benefit is that people tend to choose what they like and avoid what doesn't appeal. Funny that! However, it saves you from worrying if it is Freddy X or Freddy X's wife that intensely dislikes tomato or swells up like a balloon from eating strawberries.

Be sure to lay the food out in groups to avoid a crocodile queue. It is better to place food at 2 small tables than using one large with drinks somewhere else.

How to Figure Out How Much Food to Serve

500 grams of spaghetti will serve 8 persons
500 grams thin sausages serves 10 persons
Allow 125 grams of cooked meat per serve
2 Slices of cake per person will suffice
3 Sandwiches per person is what professional caterers work on
An average sized tart will cut into 8 pieces
Cut in half first, then quarters, and then divide the quarters in half.
125 grams of cheese per person with savouries will suffice.
A litre of icecream serves 10 persons
500 grams of butter does for 20 persons
Turkey – 3-4kg for 4 persons (including bone weight)
        5-6kg for 8 persons
        7-8kg for 12 persons

Aim at serving **ONE LARGE DISH** rather than a number of small ones. It is much easier to manage matters this way. For example, a curry with side dishes of coconut, sultanas, nuts, cucumber and rice.

The Unexpected Visitor and an Empty Cake Tin

Why is it that the visitors decide to call just after Junior has devoured the last piece of cake or just before you had intended to go shopping.

Really, its not fair. However, here they are coming down the path towards the front door. Of course when you go to their place it is always home made cake (2 choices naturally) plus tea, coffee, hot cocoa, or maybe cold watermelon juice. No, its just not fair.

If you can, send someone else to the door while you have a quick look at the state of affairs pantry wise. Check to see if there is any bread left, any jam, or maybe some cinnamon or coconut. This recipe will suit the sweet tooths and looks good if cut into triangles or fingers. It seems to bring the 'little child' out in folks.

Toast with Jam, Cinnamon or Coconut
- Toast the bread
- Butter it
- Spread with jam (if any)
- Sprinkle with cinnamon/coconut (if none, just jam it)
- Pop under griller until browns or bubbles

Cashing In On Nostalgia

If one has certain obligations socially to return but cannot face the horror of producing an a la carte menu, try cashing in on the old fashioned after noon tea. The present wave of Nostalgia has highlighted the delightfulness of this form of entertaining. To the non cook it is doubly delightful because it is easy to manage and generally is all over within the hour.

The Old Fashioned Afternoon Tea Deal

Fetch out the best china of course.
Paper Serviettes will suffice.
Posy of flowers on the table

That fancy table cloth stuffed behind in the linen press will probably suit the occasion. Its probably the one that needs ironing. However, grin and bear with it. I can assure you this type of entertaining is the easy way out. It remains up to you to mention about dear old Aunt Agatha or the like and help the memories flow along with the cucumber sandwiches and sponge cake.

What to serve

Sponge Cake

Before you faint, I am going to suggest going down to the Home Cookery and buying an unfilled sponge. After all, it is the most economical way of acquiring one.

In each section put jam, jam/cream

Ice top thickly with whipped cream
Sprinkle jelly crystals on top (like they did in the good old days) if the impulse springs to you.

Cucumber Sandwiches

These are as much admired by Royalty as they are by us ordinary mortals. You will need thinly sliced cucumber and the same for the bread. Cut into fours and serve on a sandwich tray (if you have one) or plate. That is it, and the social obligation is met.

Plain Sailing in the Kitchen

Only the truly hopeless cook can understand the frustration of the toast burning, the jug boiling over, the kids bawling whilst someone sits behind a newspaper oblivious to it all.

To make matters worse, no one seems to (want to) understand how such a situation can come about or why the cook begins to howl with rage.
Here are some ways to beat them at their game and help matters assume the intelligence that great genius is at work by the kitchen sink.

Buy a Pop Up Toaster
One that does 4 pieces at once. Don't be tempted to settle for a cheaper 2 piece model if you want a trouble free breakfast or lunch.

A Self Switching Off Kettle is a Must
This way one will not be dashing to stop it boiling over and knock down something else in the process.

Stoves that Have Heat Sensors
These stop heat build up and boil overs. They are a cooks delight. After all, who generally ends up cleaning up after the pot has boiled over cascading its contents down into the almost inaccessible corners of the stove.

Non Stick Cookware
Nothing is more frustrating than unobliging food that persists in sticking to the container. Situations such as half cooked eggs that refuse to respond to the spatula trick and splatter all over the place can really put pressure on the normal human fuse. Non stick cookware will put an end to such nightmares.

Kitchen Slaves
In days of yore, kitchens came complete not only with pots and pans, but also with plenty of labour to help with the boring jobs. There were hands to do the grating, chopping, the washer uppers, stove attendants, fetchers and carriers and the like. Of course, the Chief Cook only did the interesting jobs and gave orders.

Did you know that today in our enlightened age such help is still available from uncomplaining servants. Of course we are more polite and have nicer names but the functions are still the same.

For example, washer uppers are now called 'dishwashers', kitchen hands respond to the name 'food processor' and when one mentions 'microwave' the old stove attendant would realise it was just a science fiction word for his old job.

It was, and still is, a good idea to keep all this help available in a visible place to ensure they do a good days work rather than slinking around dark corners and in cupboards where they can't be seen.

Making the Most of Kitchen Slaves

All this help is available to you as the chief Cook but it still remains for you to give the commands and press the buttons.

Learning to do this is only a matter of habit and once it is realized how efficient these kitchen slaves can be, I guarantee you'll be grinning from ear to ear.

Food Processors

Why bother to grate, slice, dice etc when Food Processor will willingly and quickly do the chore for you. Anyhow, it is easier on your nails this way.

Watermelon juice can be made in a blender (minus the seeds of course) while turning out pancake batter and mixing cakes becomes simple and easy.

Microwaves

Who wants to sit around in the kitchen when there are so many interesting things to do in life.

It really does pay to go and have lessons. One gets to know all the tips and tricks so quickly this way. It really is a new way of cooking that makes life a lot simpler.

Blenders

Rather an indispensible little helper who never complains. It will do all sorts of fabulous tricks to make life easier in the kitchen. For example, throw in some eggs, milk, parsley, press the button and the result is instant scrambled egg waiting to be poured into a hot frypan.

Naturally, it will dig a little deeper into the hip pocket for these items. Try to purchase them one by one and then get into the swing of using them constantly. In the long run it will be cheaper than paper tissues to mop up the tears and asprins to soothe fevered brows over kitchen disasters.

To Serve with Flair

Its all very well for ardent cooks to spend time making food appealing by cutting vegetables into delicate shapes or by adding aspic. I suppose for them it is just as well we enjoy eating food presented with such flair.

To suggest the awful notion to a non cook that perhaps the same could be emulated at, well you know what address, would be as if doomsday was on the horizon.

However, all is not lost. There are some quick and easy ways to get your own back without even having to blink an eyelid.

The easiest way is:

1. *Check out the state of the kitchen crockery*

    Even cordon bleu meals would taste a little boring if served off plastic baby bowls or chipped china.

2. *Go for colour*

    Its cheap and its easy.

    For example – a slice of tomato and a piece of parsley provide extra colour: is not too taxing, and generally available in most homes.

3. *How to Serve:*

    If this conjours up visions of gracious, carefree hosts or hostesses, then promptly forget them. This isn't for you. People often remember the happiness and conversation over a meal than the food that was served. Even a simple meal of bread and cheese on a bare planked table complete with a bowl of country flowers can linger in the mind as a memorable occasion.

    Remember however, that eating with a heap of junk on the end of the table and the radio or T.V. bellowing out really does dim the gastric juices.

4. *Where to Eat:*
Restaurants are well aware of this and strive to create an atmosphere that will draw patrons.
Somehow food tastes better in different locations. Beetroot will be eaten by children in a friends house. The same beetroot can be refused at the child's own home. This even carries on to adult hood. For example tea and scones in the garden appeals far more than tea and scones during the busy work break.

How to Read These Recipies

Its amazing how quickly the cooking hour arrives and somehow has to be squeezed into the schedule. This normally happens when the cook is tired, half way through something far more exciting or emotionally unprepared to wage war with pots and pans.
You will notice there are no big lists of ingredients.
This is because they have been designed for busy people like yourself who probably want a quick and nourishing meal without the chance of too much going wrong.

Basic Recipe
This means more or less stick to the formula to save having a disaster.
If it says 'an egg' it really does mean 'an egg'

Add Any of the Following
This means search the fridge for the dash that enhances. There are quite a few alternatives because everyone knows that grocery shopping is nearly as dreadful as having to spend all that time in the kitchen. Often the result is some purchase being forgotten.
Its up to you what you choose from the list.
Maybe, its more to the point to say, choose on the list what is in your larder.
Its a bit like choosing an ice cream.
Today it may be strawberry that adds the flavour while tomorrow chocolate may take your fancy.

This gives you a chance to CREATE MORE THAN ONE VARIETY FROM THE BASIC RECIPE without having to look up half a dozen different recipies.
Most of the meals listed are not only easy to prepare. They are light on the pocket.

Index

29 **Meals with Meat**
Shepherds Pie
Chinese Style Pork/Veal
Savoury Self Cook Chops
Mince Sauce & Variations
Mince with Flair
Risotto
Curry
Sausages in Sauce
All in Together
Savoury Pies
Meals in a Bowl
Lasagne The Easy Way

51 **Meals Without Meat**
Tasty N Hasty
Three Shots at the Jackpot
Easy Bake
Potato Casserole
Saturday Lunch
Potato Fritters
Savoury Pancakes
Easy Pizza
Macaroni
Meals in a Parcel
Vegetable Loaf
Ways to Dress up
   Cooked Chook
Soup with Variations

70 **Sweetmeats**
Stand by Sauces
Cherry/Choc Squares
No Fuss Chocolate Squares
Gingernuts
White Christmas
Shortbread

76 **Desserts**
Fruit Sago
Easy Trifle N Fruit
Pavlova
Custard and Variations
Hot Apple Pudding
Pancakes

86 **Miscellaneous**

Relatively Foolproof Menu
Easy N Healthy Breakfast
Emergency Phone Numbers

Meals With Meat

Statistical figures indicate that English speaking nations consume quite an astronomical amount of meat per person over the period of one year.

Whilst this can be quite enjoyable, it can deeply touch the hip pocket nerve.

These recipies are tasty, economical both in terms of cash, and energy input.

Index

    Shepherds Pie
    Chinese Style Pork/Veal
    Savoury Self Cook Chops
    Mince Sauce & Variations
    Mince with Flair
    Risotto
    Curry
    Sausages in Sauce
    All in Together
    Savoury Pies
    Meals in a Bowl
    Lasagne the Easy Way

Shepherds Pie

I don't know if it really was Shepherds who made this dish so popular. What I can tell you is that kids generally polish it off no sweat.

Basic Recipe (For 4 Average Appetites)

About 500 Grams of Mince
2 Cups of Water
Salt
Potatoes for Topping

Add Anything of the Following:

Flavour booster – Vegemite, Bonox, Oxo Cubes
Onion
Carrot minced or diced
Peas
Tomato
1 Cup of Breadcrumbs or thereabouts

Put the basic recipe in a saucepan
Cook till mince changes colour
Add from the **Anything of the Following** List
Thicken with flour/breadcrumbs if needed
Place in a greased oven to table dish

Topping

Cook and Mash Potatoes
Drain most of the water away
Mash – will be quite stiff
   (This makes topping crisp)
If you wish – add grated cheese to potato

Place topping on mince
Put in oven for about 15 minutes at approximately 180 degrees

Chinese Style Pork/Veal

Easy to cook and doesn't create a high pile of dishes in the sink to wash up afterwards.
Will serve 4 medium appetites.

Basic Recipe (For 4 Average Appetites)

**500 Grams cubed Pork/Veal
or Pork and Veal together
2 Onions diced
2 Tomatoes diced
½ Capsicum sliced
4 Tabs Plum Sauce (Gives Oriental Flavour – buy at Grocer)
1½-2 cups Water
Dob of Butter/Oil/Marg**

Add Anything of the Following:

**Shell noodles
Macaroni
Black Pepper**

Place all ingredients (except water & noodles) in frypan/wok on medium heat
Stir till all mixed together and meat sealed
Add water – 1½-2 Cups
Add noodles if using
Place lid on
Cook for about 20 minutes
Check Occasionally

Savoury Self Cook Chops

Ever staggered home after a hard days work simply longing for a rest and a good square meal to appear on the table without a pot slinging match in the kitchen.
Help could be at hand with this recipe.

Basic Recipe No. 1

**2 Loin Chops (Lamb) per average appetite
Mustard – any sort
Bay Leaves
Tomato Paste/Sauce**

Cook either in a 180 degrees oven
Or on medium heat on the stove

Grease dish
Pack in chops
Mix 1 teas mustard and ½ cup tomato paste/sauce diluted with water for each 6 chops
Place lid on
Simmer for 1¼ hours

Hopeless Cooks Hint

This gives time for a long bath and some relaxation.
* "Smart Cookies" have been known to place (unpeeled) scrubbed spuds (whole or cut in half if large) on top of the meat to steam.
* Bayleaves come from a tree but are sold via Grocery outlets. Look in the spice department.

Savoury Self Cook Chops

Use either pork or lamb chops. Sausages taste good as well. They will need to be parcooked in water first. When you look at the list of ingredients you may wonder but I can assure you the taste buds will give you the 'thumbs up' for flavour.

Basic Recipe

1 Onion chopped
2 or 3 Apples/or Tinned Apples
Chops – 2 or 3 per person
1 Dessertspoon Vinegar
A little amount of Water

Layer – chops, apples, onion, sugar sprinkled, some of the vinegar until dish is full
Add a little amount of water to moisten.

Either – put on stove on medium heat with meat packed in a saucepan or frypan, place lid on and cook for about 1 hour. You won't need to turn the meat.
Or – put in an ovenware dish and place in 180 degrees oven for about 1 hour.

Mince Sauce

This can be used in an interesting number of ways.
Try to make double because it only takes a little extra effort but takes the load off you when preparing for another (yes another) meal.
This basic recipe is enough for 6 average appetites.

Basic Recipe

500 Grams Mince
2 Stock Cubes (flavour boosters)
3 Cups Water
Small Can Tomato Paste

Add Any of the Following:

Onion chopped up
Garlic
¼ Teas Oregano

Place all ingredients in a large saucepan/frypan
Stir till meat broken up
Simmer for about 1 hour

Uses:

Over spaghetti or rice – garnish with cheese, parsley or tomato

Thickened even more and served with toast

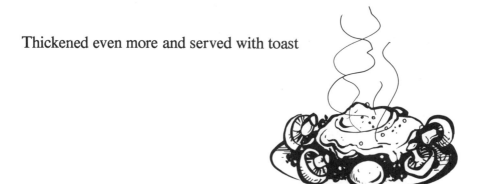

Layered with mashed potato – finish with potato and brown in oven

Thicken as a filling for savoury pie by adding pastry or bread crust.

Use as a sauce and break eggs into. One or two for each person in little hollows. Top with grated cheese and parsley. Can be done in frying pan or in the oven.

Mince With Flair & Little Effort

This is a superb looking dish that isn't fiddly. It really is a large flat rissole with a topping.

Basic Recipe

500 Grams Mince
2 Eggs (Essential to prevent crumbling & falling apart)

Add Any of the Following:

Diced Onion
Chopped Bacon
Any left over cooked Veges
Cooked Rice

Mix together
Grease very well in a frying pan then flour it
Press in Mince
Cook gently until mince turns colour
DO NOT TURN OVER
Add Topping

TOPPING

Spread with either:
Tomato Sauce/Barbeque Sauce
Tomato Paste
Tomato Slices
Chutney

THEN ADD:

Liberal amount of grated cheese

Put lid on pan and when cheese well & truly melted, serve in wedges
Eat with cooked vegetables or salad

Risotto

Add some chook and this dish becomes "Chicken Risotto". Ham makes it "Ham Risotto". In reality, the possibilities are endless.

As you can see, it is quite a versatile recipe leaving the alternatives up to you or more precisely up to what is still sitting on the shelves after the "Fridge Raiding Gang" have struck.

Basic Recipe (For 6 Average Appetites)

Risotto
1 Onion Chopped
½ Cup Raw Rice per person
½ Cup Water per person
Flavour Booster

Add Any of the Following:

½ Cup Frozen Veges per person
Celery
Bacon Pieces
1 Dessertspoon Pineapple Pieces per person
Capsicum
Mushrooms
Meat – About ½ Cup per person of either
– Diced Ham, Chook, Sausage, Pork, Lamb

In a saucepan place a dob of butter/marg/oil/bacon rind or fat
Add onion, and rice
Stir till well coated and sizzling. (Important)
Add water

Throw anything from the **Add Any of the Following** List
Simmer for about 30 minutes (white rice), for 60 minutes (brown rice)

Hopeless Cook Hint

Use a medium stove heat and keep the lid on the saucepan
Put the timer on about 20 minutes and check the water level. Add more if needed
Reset timer – then go off and enjoy yourself till it rings again

Sweet Curry

These are a good standby and can liven up any dish without too much effort. What is so good about it is that any kind of meat (or noodles etc) can be used. Since you probably know all this anyhow, I will mention that this recipe can be used for boiled eggs to cover situations such as no meat on your Refrigerator shelves, the football team with their big appetites arrive, or that your budget simply will not stretch to providing meat.

This will cover 6 normal appetites especially when rice is added as a side dish.

Note – Curry dishes improve when left over night and then reheated. In other words, if one makes too much, tomorrows left overs will taste delicious.

Basic Recipe

Dob Butter/Marg/Oil
About 2 Tabs Flour to thicken if necessary
2 Onions
1 Cup Milk soured with 1 Tab Vinegar
 (makes all the difference)
2 Dessertspoon Curry
1 Teas Ginger (optional but makes a difference)
5-6 Tabs Apricot Jam
About 5 Cups of Water

Add Any of the Following:

½ Packet Frozen Veges/Stir Fry
Coconut ½-¾ Cup
Diced Apple (skin and all)
Sultanas – handful
Tinned Pineapple
Capsicum
Meat – Chicken Pieces, Beef Cubed, Prawns, Boiled Eggs, Sausages
Cooked Macaroni if no meat

Cook onions in butter/marg/oil
Add curry powder
Then jam
Put in ginger
Add water and soured milk
Then add from *Anything of the Following* list – your choice
Simmer together till everything is cooked

Sausages in Sauce

Take a common sausage and turn it into something special and all with hardly any effort on your part at all.
Sausages are easy on the purse, especially with a crowd or if a known 'hungry horse' will be coming along.
You really do need all these bits and pieces but the taste is great!
If you want more sauce, double, or treble this recipe.

Basic Recipe (For 5 Thin Sausages)

3 Tabs Tomato Paste
2 Teas Worcestershire (or similar) Sauce
1 Teas dry Mustard   Mix Together
2 Teas Vinegar
1 Tabs Sugar – brown for preference

Simmer sausages in water for 10 minutes first. (This cooks them & helps hold the shape)
Drain
Add Sauce mixture
Bake in a Moderate (180 degrees C) oven for about 20 minutes

Serve with any of the following if you wish
Rice, spaghetti, noodles
Vegetables
Salad

All in Together

This is a simple but nutritious cure for hunger pains. It won't take a lot of energy on your part nor will it call for a University Degree to work out the ingredients or how to put them together.
What is so good about it is that double can be made with only a little extra effort on your part to store in the deep freeze for use later on.

If you own a crockpot, super. If not, simply use a heavy based (a must) pan on low heat (another must).

Brown both sides of the meat. Add onion, water and tomato.
Turn stove onto low and put lid on saucepan.
It will take about 2 hours.

It won't hurry matters up by turning the stove higher unless you wish to give teeth sharpening lessons to enable everyone to chew the meat.
Its the low, slow cooking that tenderises the meat. It will take about 2 hours prior to mealtime to cook which means something else can be done in the meantime.
If possible, stir about every 30 minutes. Put a timer on as a reminder. If necessary, add more water.

Basic Recipe

All in Together
Meat – either Lamb Chops, Skirt or Barbeque Steak
Gauge the quantity for each diner
Onion
Tomato
About a Cup of Water
A dob of Butter/Oil Marg

About 30 minutes before serving up, add from *Any of the Following* list.

Add Any of the Following:

**Parsnip, Carrot, Tomato,
Macaroni, Rice,
Large pieces of Pumpkin, Potato (smaller goes to mash)
Flavour boosters such as Oxo Cube, Gravy Maker, sauce,**

Savoury Pies

The shops are shut, tea time is nearly upon you and, oh dear, there doesn't seem much alternative than to A: Pretend feeding time doesn't exist B; Takeaways.
Well cheer up, here is an almost foolproof pie crust that can take any sort of filling and before a case of dramatics threatens to engulf, let me assure you, it is simple, quick and easy to make.
It can also be used for a pizza base.

Basic Recipe
½ Cup Oil or Melted Marg/Butter
½ Cup Water
2-2½ Cups Self Raising Flour
(or 1 Cup Self Raising Flour,
1 cup Plain Flour is even better)

Add Oil/Marg to water
Mix with Flour

Press into a greased pie dish – don't use a rolling pin – no need
Forget about a lid for the pie – looks better without anyhow
If you do get carried away and want to garnish, sprinkle with breadcrumbs or slices of buttered bread (with butter upwards)

Put in Filling
Cook for about 20 minutes at 200 degrees

Put pie in an oven on 200 degrees whilst sorting out the filling.
(This stops it being soggy in the middle)

Suggested Fillings

What you put in as a filling decides what it will be called. For example, mince pie has mince, egg and bacon pie has exactly that.

So, once you know how to make a simple pastry (without too much effort of course), the sky is the limit.

1. Left over Veges in white sauce
2. Egg and Bacon
3. Tinned Fish in white sauce
4. Egg and Cheese
5. Mince

1. Left over Veges in White Sauce

In a saucepan on stove put:
1 Tab Butter/Marg
2 Tabs Flour
Cook till forms a ball
Add about 2 Cups Milk
About Cup Grated Cheese
Add left over veges
P.S. Better to be too thick than runny.

2. Egg and Bacon

Allow ½ rasher bacon per person (cut up and fat trimmed)
Allow 1 egg per person
Crack eggs into pastry and break up with a fork
Add bacon
That's the big deal

3. Tinned Fish

Same as with veges but use fish instead

4. Egg and Cheese

Takes a bit more work so save it until you feel noble, have a food processor, or until some unsuspecting victim wanders in to do the grating : have been smart enough to buy the cheese grated.
250 grams grated cheese
3 eggs
Add Any of the Following
Bacon bits
Corn
Frozen mixed vegetables
It will look a but messy but really cooks up a feast fit for a king.

5. Mince

In a saucepan, place the Mince
Add some water
Add any veges if wish
Flavour booster (Oxo Cube, Vegemite)
Thicken with Flour or handful of Breadcrumbs
(Breadcrumbs 'stretch' the meat and really make a meat pie very tasty. No one seems to suspect.

P.S. Smart Cookies use a clear pyrex pie dish so they can see if the base is cooked through (goes brown).

Meals in a Bowl

The correct culinary name for this dish is chowder. To the non cook the term really means serving a decent nutritious meal in a bowl (or soup mug) with hardly any washing up strewn around the sink area.

Basic Recipe

1 Onion sliced
2 Cups Veges – your choice
2 Cups Milk
Meat – Your Choice – about 1 cup
    Chook cooked
    Ham
    Salmon
    Fresh Fish Cubed
    Bacon

Fry onion in marg/butter/oil
Add meat and veges
Then milk
Thicken with flour if necessary

Lasagne – The Easy Way

Let the Supercooks sigh over how fiddly it is to make this superb dish. Lasagne, they say, takes a lot of preparation, accompanied naturally with a loud sigh. What they don't know is some slick tricks to reduce it all to an assembly line job. Of course they won't approve so if they ask for the recipe, smirk and say its a secret.

Basic Recipe (for 4 hearty appetites)

Mince Part

**About 450 grams Mince
or Mince & Breadcrumbs
Tomato Paste and Water mixed totalling 2 cups**

Put all in a saucepan on the stove
Cook till turns brown

Sauce Part

**1 Cup Cream
1 Cup Milk
2 Cups Grated Cheese
About ½ Teas Nutmeg – makes the difference**

Mix all together

Lasagne Part:

Use PRECOOKED LASAGNE

How to Assemble:
Layer – Mince Part
      Sauce Part
      Sheets of Pre Cooked Lasagne

Finish with the Sauce Part
Put in oven for 30 minutes on 180 degrees

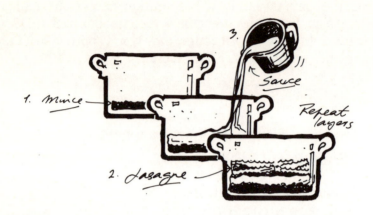

Hopeless Cook Hint

You will think it all looks a bit runny. This is the secret to a moist lasagne.
Proof will be in the eating.

— •• —

Meals Without Meat

It would be a rare household that eats meat every night of the week, so relax, it really is quite normal to serve something else without A. Feeling that times are hard, B. You really are not a good manager.
Besides all this unless one has shares in the Meat Factory, it can really chew into the household budget to buy meat all the time.
Here is a list of recipes to help get you started and to make life easier.

Index
    Hasty N Tasty
    3 Shots at the Jackpot
    Easy Bake
    Potato Casserole
    Saturday Lunch
    Potato Fritters
    Savoury Pancakes
    Easy Pizza
    Macaroni
    Meals in a Parcel
    Vegetable Loaf
    Chook and Ways to Dress Up
    Soup

Hasty and Tasty

Ideal for a snack or when time is short.

Basic Recipe (For 4 Hearty Appetites)

2 Cups Mashed Potato
3 Eggs
1 Cup of Grated Cheese

Add Any of the Following:

Make total up to 1½ cups of:
Peas
Carrots
Tomato
Celery
Mushrooms
Chopped Cooked Meat
Hint of Mustard

Mix together
Place in a greased ovenware dish
Bake for 30 minutes at 200 degrees

Mornay – 3 Shots at the Jackpot

I'd like to call this recipe Three Shots at the Jackpot as it gives you alternatives, depending what is left in the Larder.
It will also determine whether it is called:
Fish Mornay using about a 400 gram tin of tuna
Chicken Mornay a good cupful of chicken cooked
Asparagus Mornay using about a 400 gram tin of asparagus

Basic Recipe

2 Tabs Plain Flour
Large Dob of Butter (about 1 heaped tab)
1 Cup Milk – ½ Cup liquid from tins
　or 1½ Cups Milk
2 Tabs Breadcrumbs
¼-½ Cup Grated Cheese

Then Add Any of the Following:

Fish Mornay – tin of Tuna/Salmon, Onion
Chicken Mornay – Mushrooms, Corn, Chicken
Asparagus Mornay – Asparagus

Cook flour and butter till forms a ball
Add liquids and stir (like a custard)
Add cheese
Thicken again with the breadcrumbs

Then serve up –
To keep hot for a while – put in a greased oven dish sprinkle with breadcrumbs and grated cheese – delicious!
Serves 3 medium appetites

Easy Bake

Simple as falling off a log but tastes as if it took hours of preparation.

Basic Recipe

1 Cup Self Raising Flour (or 1 Cup Plain with 1 Teas Baking Powder)
1 Egg
1 Onion
About ½ Cup Water
1 Cup Grated Cheese
1 Cup Bacon Pieces or Corn

Two Choices on How to Cook:

1. Mix together and put on a greased tray in oven for 25 minutes at 180 degrees.

2. Put a fair drop of marg/bacon fat/oil in frypan on medium heat. Add mixture and cook on medium heat for about 20 minutes. Don't turn over.
To crisp up top (if you simply must), pop under griller.

Serves 4 medium appetites

Potato Casserole

Only the Hopeless Cook can really understand how: the cupboards look so bare: shopping be a drudgery: producing luscious, tasty yet nutritious meals becomes an unbelievable horror.
Besides, there are so many other exciting things to do, read and go to see, yet meals still have to be cooked. Winter just seems to make matters worse.
This recipe shouldn't tax your strength too much and one can even do something far more exciting whilst it is obediently cooking in the oven.

Basic Recipe

5 good sized Spuds par boiled and sliced
(Don't peel, simply wash well)
4 Tomatoes sliced
2 Onions sliced
3 Cups Cheese grated (or sliced)
1 Cup Milk

Add Any of the Following:

For Tomato haters – omit and replace with corn
Parsley
Broccoli – par boiled
Eggs to fortify the Milk

Grease ovenware
Layer ingredients starting with spuds and ending with cheese
Pour over milk or milk fortified with eggs
Cook at 180 degrees a minimum of 30 minutes. If you require 45 minutes it will still end up an appetising dish!

Saturday Lunch (Savoury Brown Lentils)

Sick of baked beans or spaghetti?
Savoury brown lentils and rice combined could ring a pleasant change and also provide the 22 amino acids that form a perfect protein. This being the case, you can feel virtuous as well as adventurous.

Basic Recipe

1 Cup of Brown Lentils
½ Cup of Rice
About 2 Cups of Water

Add Any of the Following:

Chopped Onion
Any other Vege that takes your fancy or graces cupboard shelves such as:-
Corn
Celery
Peas
Capsicum in small amounts
Vegemite or flavour booster

If there is any left over mashed spuds, toss lentils into a greased ovenware and top with the mashed spuds, rather like a shepherds pie.
Generally takes about 30-40 minutes (without presoaking) for lentils to cook.
Thicken if necessary.
There you are, all in one pot. By the way, if you find the rice is still on the grocer's shelf and not yours, use macaroni instead or simply omit altogether.

Potato Fritters

By the time Friday night is in sight, no one in their right minds would dream of cooking a full orbed meal if they can get out of it. ·
Besides all that, it does seem to herald the weekend to do 'something different'. Provided of course, that 'something different' isn't 'something complicated'.
Potato Fritters seems to fit the bill nicely: not difficult and yet infinitely more nutritious than takeaways.

Basic Recipe

Grated Potato – allow 1 per person
Egg – allow 1 per person

Mix together
Cook in frypan that has plenty of butter/marg/oil in it
Note – It will look gloppy whilst cooking but I can assure you that the taste is great

For Special Occasions:

To feed a crowd, as they are made place on a tray in the oven until sufficient quantity is made.
To dress up:
Add Any of the Following:

Chopped Onion
Parsley
Crumbled Bacon Cubes

Pancakes (Makes 4 medium sized pancakes)

Admittedly a little more fiddly than the other recipies. However, it does make up for this when there is not much of anything else around to eat. Everything can be mixed together to make a filling.
Besides, some cooks spend hours cutting up bits of this and bits of that for variety and here it is all waiting simply because one has had to postpone the grocery shopping.

Basic Recipe

(This makes Pancakes for both sweet and savoury)
1 Cup Plain Flour
1 Egg
1 Cup Milk (water will work if no milk)

Savoury Filling:
Add Any of the Following:
Zuccini,
Pumpkin
Potato
Tomato
Onion
In fact almost any type of Vege
Left Over Meat
Curry the lot if you wish

Mix basic recipe together – Blenders are ideal for this
Well grease a fry pan and put over medium heat (or else you will have pancakes burnt one side and raw in the middle)
Pour the (thinnish looking) pancake mix into pan – enough to cover the base of pan
When it looks set and firm – turn
Brown the other side

Easy Pizza

Pizzas are really easy this way, a lot cheaper and nicer than bought ones.
For a filling pizza use wholemeal flour. Your body will appreciate it.
Always make a large one: cut in half if need be and freeze for next time. It saves a lot of work for the next occasion.
Pizza trays with holes in the base are the best as they help the base to cook and gives the cook a view of how brown it is.

Basic Recipe

Base
½ Cup Oil
½ Cup Water
2-2½ Cups Self Raising Flour
(1 Cup Self Raising, balance Plain Flour is even better)
Basic Filling
Tomato Paste diluted with water
Grated Cheese

Add Any of the Following:
Pineapple
Salami
Mushrooms
Onion
Anything you fancy

Mix Base ingredients together in a bowl
Grease a tray

Place on base on tray in dobs and push together

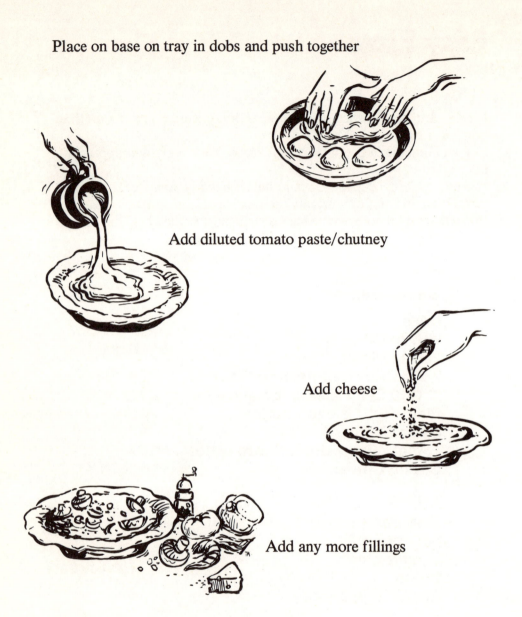

Add diluted tomato paste/chutney

Add cheese

Add any more fillings

Place in oven 210 degrees for 20 minutes
Set the Timer

Hopeless Cook Hint

Smart Cookies have discovered that a thick layer of chutney plus the cheese will give all the flavours with a lot less effort on your part.

Macaroni

Really very easy to make and just as easy to eat.
Hint Cook macaroni in water, drain and then add ingredients to the pot.
This saves dirtying another bowl.

Basic Recipe

1 Cup Macaroni Cooked
1 Cup Grated Cheese
2 Eggs
1 Cup Milk
About ½ Cup Breadcrumbs

Add Any of the Following:

Mushrooms
Corn
Bacon Pieces
Onion Diced
Peas
Parsley
Dob of Butter/Cream

Mix together
Place in a greased ovenware dish for about 15 minutes at 180 degrees.

Note – To really jazz up for a special occasion, top with par-cooked bacon strips and slices of tomato before putting in oven.

Meals in a Parcel

Cooks Night Off Special
This is so easy it shouldn't tax anyones brain.
Note – Puffed pastry is generally stored in the deep freeze both at home and at the local supermarket.

Basic Recipe

**1 Sheet frozen Puffed pastry per person
    (Smaller appetites share 1 parcel)
Left overs from fridge such as:
    Meat and Veges
    Cheese and Baked Beans
    Eggs and Bacon
    Anything Savoury that appeals**

1

Put oven on 200 degrees.

2

Lay out sheets and let thaw a minute

3

Put a largish blob of filling on each sheet

4

Wrap up, as would fish and chips

5

Grease an Ovenware dish Put in oven

6

Prick (to let steam out) – don't forget!

7

Put timer on 30 minutes

8

Hang around so you can hear the bell on the timer.

Eat.

Vegetable Loaf

Actually it only takes a jiffy in a food processor. Simply put the grated's all together and then its simply a matter of chucking in the liquid, eggs and breadcrumbs.
If no food processor, wait for an unsuspecting victim to wander into the kitchen, especially one who owes you a favour.

Basic Recipe

About 1 Cup Grated Carrot (that is 2 medium sized carrots)
About 2 Cups Grated Potato (that is 2 medium sized spuds)
About ½ Cup Liquid – Preferably Milk
3 Eggs
About 1 Cup of Breadcrumbs (or grated bread)
About 1 Cup Grated Cheese

Add Any of the Following:

Mushrooms
Smoked Meat/Salami/Bacon
Sauce

Mix well
Put in greased oven dish
Cook for Minimum of 60 minutes at 180 degrees

Don't bother to peel the veges as most of the nutrition is just under the skin. Simply wash well.

Hopeless Cook Hint

It really does take the hour for the veges to cook. Actually, its just long enough to take a reviving plunge in the bath tub and have a few minutes relaxing (while the food cooks all by itself in the oven.)

To Cook a Chook

It really is a job for the Chicken Bar and seeing they are so expert at it, why not let them continue doing it.
Everyone knows it is almost as cheap as doing it yourself and besides, they have the job of cleaning out the dirty oven instead of you.

Ways to Dress up a Cooked Chook:

1. Chicken in Curry   Page 41

Make the curry and pour over the chicken portions as sauce.

2. Chicken Chowder   Page 48

Ideal for using up odd slices or pieces of chook. It does stretch a meal when the pickings are light on.

3. Chicken Risotto   Page 38

Makes a change. What this really means is that chicken can be served more often as the emphasis is on the other ingredients. If anyone does comment on "Chicken Again?", simply assume a very intelligent pose and reply that the meat from chicken is polyunsaturated in fats and therefore tends to avoid the clogging of the arteries in the body. Its a case of using the "Dazzle 'em with science trick".

4. Chicken Mornay   Page 53

This will suit all manner of occasions and look the part. It is as comfortable as a wedding breakfast dish as it is in the family meal situation.

5. Chicken with Lemon Sauce

Take the chook out of the bag and pull into portions.
Pour the following sauce over and place in oven/frying pan for about 20 minutes

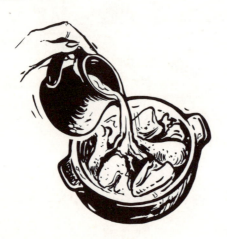

2 Teas Worcestershire/Soy Sauce
¼ Cup Oil
⅓ Cup Lemon Juice and some Rind (if possible)
1 Tab Honey
Mix together and pour over

Soup

Everyone knows that soup comes out of a can or a packet. However, there is another method of making soup that produces excellent results, is far more nutritious and is simple enough for even the most ardent non cook to make.

It is called "Home Made Method". Its main advantages besides cheapness, are that it contains no preservatives, colourants etc that are not the best for anyone's body. Besides, the flavour is unbelievable!

Basic Recipe

Soup Bones – either bacon bones, ham bones or chicken carcasses
Water – plenty of it
Vegetables
Pulses

Always use a large pot and plenty of water over the bones (The idea is to cook slowly and for a long time to extract nutrients from the bones. It will takes ages, in fact hours. It will look a bit off putting but this is the part that creates the goodness)

Add some time during simmering:-

Pulses – that is either:
Lentils
Soup Grain Mix
Split green/yellow peas

Towards the end of cooking process:-

Any vegies that take your fancy
Noodles
Flavour Booster (if you think its needed)

Variations

Bacon bones and Split green peas – called Pea and Ham Soup
Ham Bones and Split green/yellow peas – called Pea and Ham Soup

Hopeless Cooks Hint

Soup is easy to freeze and a handy standby. In fact it takes 3 cookings to really get all the nutrition out of the bones, so don't be tempted to fish them out and put them in the garbage.

About freezing- freeze in meal portions rather than in one large container unless of course you fancy a litre or so of soup for a snack.

Pumpkin Soup

Sounds posh and yet is very easy to make. It should impress most visitors as well as satisfying a hungry family.
This recipe should serve 4 medium appetites.
If possible, use a Jarradale Pumpkin, but any pumpkin is O.K.

Basic Recipe

1½ Cups Mashed Pumpkin
1½ Cups Milk
Dash of Nutmeg ⎫
1 Chicken Cube ⎭ Makes all the difference

Mix Together

Reheat *slowly* together.
If the blender is available, chuck the lot in and let it do the work for you.

To Serve with Flair

Add cream and milk to make about 1½ cups
Chopped parsley can be stirred through
A slice of orange on top looks impressive

Sweetmeats

Why is it those exciting invitations often have in small writing 'Please bring a plate'. Its not the fact of having to bring anything but the thought of what the Supercooks will bring on their plate that is the trouble.
Of course its not fair to little ol' you, but with these simple recipes not only will you bring a 'plate' but collect a handful of compliments as well.
I promise you they are not too hard or complicated and certainly will not take long to make.

Index

Cherry/Choc Squares
No Fuss Chocolate Squares
Gingernuts
White Christmas
Shortbread

Cherry/Choc Squares

Basic Recipe

250 Grams Cooking Chocolate melted
About 45 Grams Copha/Marg/Butter melted
        or
350 Grams Cooking Chocolate
1½ Cups Coconut
125 Gram Packet Glace Cherries cut up
   (into 4's is good)
1 Packet biscuits broken into nibble size

Mix Together
Press into a flatish container
Store in fridge

To Serve with Flair:

Top with melted chocolate
Cut into Diamond shape

Hopeless Cook Hint

These can be stored in the deep freeze to hinder the Fridge Raiding Gang.
Cut into squares first. Take out of Freezer just before required.

No Fuss Chocolate Squares

This is superb, rather sophisticated and no one would guess that all your skills and time has not been put to the test.

Basic Recipe

Melt 4 oz (125 Grams) Butter/Marg
Add 2 Tabs Sugar
Add 1½ Tabs Cocoa
1 Egg
1 Packet of Crushed Biscuits

Add Any of the Following if Wish

Cut up Glace Cherries
Walnuts/Nuts Crushed
Dash of Rum

Melt Basic Recipe in a saucepan on the stove.

Stir Constantly or else it will be scrambled eggs!

Add Crushed Biscuits plus your choice from the Any of the Following List.
Mix Together
Line a dish with alfoil/cling wrap (to make removal easier)
Place mixture in dish
Ice if wish
Add a warning sign to discourage fridge raiding gang

Gingernuts

This should make 3 weeks supply of biscuits without 3 lots of effort on your part.
It really is a sneaky recipe because the Fridge Raiding Gang cannot crunch through them in the first week. The reason for this is because frozen biscuit dough doesn't seem to raise much enthusiasm in them.
What happens is that the following mixture is made up and then rolled into 3 sausages.
Do this by laying some plastic film (or aluminium foil) down and rolling the dough up in the shape of a long sausage. In fact, 3 long sausages will represent 3 lots of biscuits.
Then sling them in the deep freeze for safe keeping.
When wishing to make up into delicious mouth watering cookies, slice up the 'sausage of dough' whilst frozen and pop into a preheated oven at 180 degrees for about 10 minutes.

Basic Recipe

250 Grams Butter/1 Cup Oil
1 Egg
1½ Cups Sugar
2 Tabs Golden Syrup
2 Teas Baking Soda
2 Teas Ginger
2 Teas Cinnamon (don't fret if omitted)
2 Teas Grated Orange Peal (don't fret if omitted)
3½ Cups Self Raising Flour

In a bowl, mix together. Add Flour 1 cup at a time to make life easier.
Roll the (stiffish) dough into sausages.
Either cook immediately or store in deep freeze until ready to use.

White Christmas

This is as simple as falling off a log and yet quite a treat to eat.

Basic Recipe

8 oz Copha/Margarine – melted
1 Cup full each of: Mixed Fruit
                      Coconut
                      Icing Sugar
                      Powdered Milk
2 Cups of Rice Bubbles

Mix together
Press in a tray, preferably greased
Cut into squares
Store in fridge

Shortbread

I don't think you ever will find an odd piece of shortbread disregarded in the biscuit tin. It is a versatile sweetmeat that is acceptable on all levels of social occasions.
The way the word was mentioned, one could assume it is difficult to make.
This recipe should help you hold your head up high and receive compliments whilst all the time you are trying to keep a naughty grin to yourself because you know how simple it was to make.

Basic Recipe
250 Grams Butter/Marg
¾ Cup of Icing Sugar
3 Cups of Plain Flour

Put all the basic recipe in a food processor till it resembles small breadcrumbs.
   or
Thumb butter through flour if no food processor. Then add sugar.
Grease a tray
Press mixture in.
Note – It will look crumbly but press in about 20mm (¾") thick. Press rather hard till it firms up – the high butter content does this.
Cut into squares before cooking.
Put in oven about 150 degrees for about 35 minutes.

To Serve with Flair
After cutting into squares/fingers either:
   Sprinkle with sugar
   Place a chocolate drop or 2 on each square

Desserts

Its not very healthy to make them you know. The pity of it is that no one else seems to agree with you. after all, seeing they do not offer to help out, why should they complain?

However, if the occasion does demand some action on your part, here are some recipes that are as simple as falling off a log and will keep everyone happy.

Mind you, remind them it is a treat that will appear only once in a while ... a long while.

Index
    Fruit Sago
    Easy Trifle and Fruit
    Pavlova
    Custard and Variations
    Hot Apple Pudding
    Pancakes

Fruit Sago

This is an old timer that is quite acceptable and very versatile.
This will cater for 4 average diners. For a larger quantity simply multiply.

Basic Recipe

½ Cup Sago
3 Cups Water

Add any of the Following:

Jam – about 3 Tabs
Sugar to sweeten
Passionfruit
Pineapple
Tin of Fruit Salad/or Apricots/Blackberries etc.
Fresh fruit any variety chopped up
Fruit – dried, fresh plus Coconut

In a Saucepan put sago and water on a low heat
It will take about 30 minutes to thicken and go clear
As it takes about this long, it gives you time to have a cup of coffee and scan the newspaper. The big 'but' is that you must stand by the stove and do these activities so you don't forget to stir.
When the little balls go clearish, add the *Any of the Following* List.

Easy Trifle N Fruit

This is just so easy I'm sure you could just about manage it with your eyes shut.

Basic Recipe

1 Packet of Gingernuts
1 Tin of Fruit – Apples, Peaches, Pears are good
1 Bottle of Cream whipped
   or 1½ Cups Milk

Assemble in Layers
Gingernuts
Cream
Fruit
Repeat till dish filled
Finish with cream

That's the big deal!

To Serve with Flair:
Use a See Through Dish so the layers are obvious.

Pavlova

This dessert is as acceptable to the Director of the largest Company as it is to the newest clerk.

The fact that is is so disgustingly easy to make is really too boring even to mention.

I want to tell you *what to do* and *why you are doing it* which makes it all so simple and successful.

Why's and Wherefores
4 egg whites – no yellow specks (fish them out) or it won't beat up stiff
¾ Cup Sugar – to make the meringue outside and give sweetness
½ Teas Cream of Tartar – to make the egg whites stiffen up
1½ Teas Vinegar – to make it marshmallowy inside

Basic Recipe
4 Egg whites beaten stiff
¾ Cup White Sugar
½ Teas Cream of Tartar
1½ Teas Vinegar

Add sugar to beaten egg whites and beat again
Then add Cream of Tartar and Vinegar
Grease alfoil and make a 'nest' shape with the mixture
Place in oven 125 degrees (no higher) for 1 hour
Then turn oven off and leave till oven cooled
(It really dries the mixture out rather than cooking it)

Hopeless Cooks Hint
Don't use a plastic mixing bowl or the egg whites won't whip up stiffly.

Custard

Custard is great stuff. It can be used in endless ways and is easy to make. An extra bonus is that milk and any added eggs make it nutritious.

Kids seem to always like it as well, while older folk seem to think if its dessert, it just has to be custard.

Always make double, or treble, depending of course, on your tribe.

First time around

Add to fresh fruit (such as bananas) or tinned fruit.

None of those around? Then add a teaspoon of jam on top 'like mother used to in the good old days'. No Jam? How about cinnamon sprinkled on, coconut or even hundreds and thousands.

Second time around

Buy a sponge or use some stale cake and make a simple trifle.
Cake cubed
Custard
Fruit or Jelly
Repeat till bowl topped up
Nuts on top, or cream if you simply must or the taste buds demand it.

Third time around

Buy a plum pudding or a sponge with jam put in the middle and cut into largish squares
Put custard on top.

Beware – It isn't a good idea to let younger children make it as it can, in the case of a mishap burn badly.

Basic Recipe

2 Heaped Tabs Custard Powder
½ Cup Milk
Sugar to taste
Add to about 2½ Cups of Hot Milk

Mix to a paste

Stand by the stove (you must stir the pot) and have a hot cup of tea or coffee.
By the time it is drunk you will feel refreshed and the custard will be made.
It is tempting to turn up the heat to cook quicker. Experience teaches that it is better to be patient than to expend energy cleaning the base of burnt custard pots and wreck your nails into the bargain.

Tempting Variations that are quick:

Coconut Custard
Add coconut to custard

Chocolate Custard

1 Tab Cocoa
Will need extra Sugar

Vanilla Slices

Line dish with alfoil
Layer Saos

Put in custard (thickened even more with extra tabs of custard powder when making)
Layer of Saos

Ice – preferably with passionfruit for extra flavour
Cut into squares the size of the sao.

Chocolate Slices

Same as above using chocolate custard

Gingernut (or similar) and Custard Dessert

Place a layer of gingernut or similar biscuits in a dish
Pour on hot custard
Add coconut if you want to

Repeat layers, gingernuts, custard till bowl is full. End with custard on top.

Hot Apple Pudding

When the winds blow and the temperatures plummet, this will warm the cockles of the heart. In folks who are creeping up in years, it will cause the reminiscences to flow and the spirit of nostalgia will be reawakened.

This is great news to the Non Cook. Food that is eaten in a happy frame of mind seems to taste that so much better. Just think what nostalgia can do for you!

Basic Recipe

Sliced Apples/Tinned Apple
½ Cup Golden Syrup
1 Cup Hot Water
About 3 Slices Buttered Bread

Fill an ovenware dish ¾ full of apple
Place buttered bread on top – butter up
Pour the Golden Syrup with the hot water
over the bread and apples
Put in oven at 180 degrees for about 1 hour

Eat with custard/cream/icecream

Pan Cake Parlour Night (At Home)

This is a cheap way out when kids clamour, as most kids do, for pancakes.
Consolation for the Cook:
Think of the money that will be saved especially when eyes have ordered bigger than appetites and it ends up in the doggy bin.
Of course you deserve to spend the money you saved. No one else might agree but it is fun to work out what neat little purchase would reward you for all this effort

Basic Recipe

Makes 4 Medium Pancakes
1 Cup Plain Flour
1 Egg
1 Cup Milk (water will work if no milk)

Mix together
Grease Frypan base
Put pan on medium heat
Pour the (thinnish looking) batter into the pan
Just enough to cover the base
When it looks firm, turn over
Brown other side

Suggested Fillings:

I am sure there will be no lack of suggestions from the siblings.
However, if their ideas and imaginations are too wild for the state of the larder, resort to a game that starts off like ...."
"I would like Pancakes with a filling of ...."
The 'filling of' will be something they have espied in the pantry/fridge. The fact that it saves you worrying about thinking up ideas of what to eat would only spoil their fun if you mentioned it! After all, they think you are really being generous.

Hopeless Cook Hint

If you are very smart, eat out doors so there is no cutlery etc to wash up. Dribbles will fall on the grass which of course needs no laundering and ironing by someone (usually you.)

Standby Sauces

These are combinations that work well together.
By using different sauces one can dress up left overs and dull fare (without too much effort on your part of course) and turn out a presentable meal. For example, a sausage needn't remain a plain old snag when little ol' you knows some tricks.
Here are 3 old reliables:

Chopped/tinned apple
Onions
Brown Sugar (to sweeten)
About 1 dessertspoon Vinegar (to mellow)
Water
Thicken if needed

****

Tomatoes
Onion
Capsicum
Plum Sauce/Chutney (gives oriental flavour)
Water
Thicken if needed

****

Pineapple Juice/Fruit
Onion
Capsicum
Vinegar
Water
Thicken if needed

****

Your Own Brain Child – either worked out by your own grey matter upstairs or filched from a friend:-

A Relatively Foolproof Menu

The voice on the other end of the phone has just informed you that Mr. XYZ, the Company Manager is coming home for dinner. You are also made quite aware that there is a promotion in the air and please! ... somehow ... turn out a spectacular something to impress him.

O.K., sit down and have an indulgent cup of tea or coffee and muse how cruel your fate is. You'll then have to come back to reality because, no mistake made, they'll both turn up hale and hearty about 6 p.m. with appetites like wolf hounds.

Try this simple menu. You can't possibly go wrong (or at least I don't think you can.)

MENU:

Pea Soup
Cheese Pie and Vegetables
Apple and Cream

Hint Lay the Table first with the best china and flowers etc even if you have to lock the kids out of the house. If things get delayed, it will at least look impressive even if one has to give the guest a drink first to gain more time.

This should do six average appetites although I have known some folk to eat unbelievable amounts of the pea soup.

Pea Soup (Should be fairly thick)

1 Packet of Split Green Peas
Cover well with water
Put Lid on and cook on medium for about an hour

Then Add Any of the Following

Salt to taste
Vegemite/Bonox
Slivers of Bacon or Ham

To Serve with Flair

Cut squares of toast buttered and pop under griller for a moment

Cheese Pie

Don't bother to make a crust. Anyhow most Executives are probably glad to skip extra kilojoules.
Grease pie plate well

Basic Recipe

About 250 Grams Grated Cheese
Add 3 or 4 Eggs

Add Any of the Following

½ Cup of Milk
Not enough Cheese – then add some raw grated Potato

Note – It will look a bit sloppy but tastes great. I can also guarantee there will be no worries about it being tough as can be the case with meat.

Cook about 180 degrees but don't let it bubble. After about 45 minutes, it will be (or should be) brown and after an hour, it will puff up.

Vegetables

It will be a case of what's left in the Larder.

Potatoes – Cook and leave in large pieces if you wish. Add butter, salt or parsley if you wish. Mashing can be a lot of work.

Peas   – I bet you have some of these around

Carrots, Pumpkin if any but if desperate, slices of tomato.

To Serve with Flair:-

Serve in separate bowls on the table and let diners serve themselves.

This saves you worrying about food becoming cold while trying to attractively serve up.

Dessert (if they can fit it in)

1 tin of sliced apples (Hide the tin of course)
1 small bottle of cream whipped

To Serve with Flair:-

Mix walnuts or chocolate drops with apple (if available)
Add whipped cream
Garnish with walnut or chocolate drop

Hint – Put Pea Soup on first
Then make Cheese Pie
Then make Apple & Cream and put in fridge

Easy Healthy Breakfast

If the campaign against excess salt and sugar is getting through and you feel that something ought to be done about it ... by you, here is a simple way to deal with both your conscience and your diet.

Easy Method

This should last about 2 weeks depending on the size of the family. Throw it all together in one large bin, put a measure of a cup inside the bin and let everyone help themselves at breakfast time.

Basic Recipe

1 Packet Rolled Oats
1 Packet of Wheat Germ
1 Packet of Bran
1 Packet of Currants

Then add Any of the Following

Sultanas
Raisins
Dried Fruit
Chopped Nuts
Lecithin

Simply pour hot or cold milk, add sugar and there it is, health and wealth (much cheaper than bought variety) all wrapped up together.

The Hopeless Cook Status Quo

Its amazing how seemingly nice people can give such seemingly nice gifts to Hopeless Cooks. These gifts generally consist of such items as peppercorn grinders, graters that will cut 50 or so varied shapes, jelly moulds, etc., all of which generally generate a sense of inadequacy.

A cupboard full of these reminders of inadequacy should not be tolerated. I am sure one can find grateful recipients for them and at the same time clear the perennial mess and present a new start plus a fair deal for the Hopeless Cook.

The Hopeless Cooks Ideal Kitchen Gear:

Knives	Use only the ones you love and quit the rest including blunt ones.
Bowls	The more you have, the more washing up is created.
Ornaments	There is a tendency in Hopless Cooks to create a Cooking Image:– Biscuit Barrels, wall hangings etc, all of which need dusting and spending more time in the kitchen.
Cake Tins	Either keep 'em and use 'em or donate them.
Electric Gadgetry	Tin openers, coffee grinders, crock pots, sandwich makers. They look good but really, if they are there, someone might expect you to actually use them.

The Kitchen

It is an amazing fact that kitchens seem to attract only the cook and that sometimes not of the person's volition. However, seeing eating is such fun, it just has to be that time is spent in the kitchen preparing meals and cleaning up.

It is important that it is an appealing place to be. The experts tell us that people spend an average of 24 hours a week in the kitchen and that is a long time for any Hopeless Cook. Sometimes a little organization and redecorating can make all the difference when it comes to facing meal preparation.

The Hopeless Cook as a Person
Hopeless cooks are generally marvellous people and ... very interesting to talk to. Sure, they generally have no knowledge of how to make a sponge but can entertain with all sorts of OTHER interesting information.

Good at Making Something:
It is generally found that everyone can make one thing well. For example Sarah is a dreadful cook but makes marvellous scones. Peter hasn't stepped inside a kitchen to cook for years and yet can organize great get togethers. He concentrates on organizing other people to actually do the cooking.
After all, this is how some of the worlds famous food chains came into existance.

Keep it Simple:
Forget about the fancy stuff. Its not for Hopeless Cooks. Serve simple and wholesome food. In other words, concentrate serving with flair. Simple food will stand up well in any situation.
For example – The Mornay Recipe in this book.
As Posh Nosh – Serve in the finest china and it looks the part.
Homely Fare – Normal Household plates etc.
Entertaining – Use a pottery dish and also pottery side plates.

Fun for the Hopeless Cook:
Its easy to get stewed up about cooking especially when its brought to your attention at meal times.
However, if everyone still seems to be managing and this book has given you some ideas and help, why not take this final piece of advice.
Relax and Just Enjoy Being Yourself.

Emergency Phone Numbers

Local Takeaway

After Hours Takeaway

Good Cheap Restaurant

Friends who owe you a meal

Mother

Best Hints from Other Hopeless Cooks

Jason:
If I had to cook all the time I'd buy a year's supply of paper plates.

Sam:
A wok – It would be the same every night. Everything all in together and it would be healthy.

Anna:
Desserts – A thing of the past. If anyone insists, there's milk in the fridge, a biscuit for them and a piece of fruit.

Jo:
My best hint is soup. A big potful made on the weekend and frozen into meal portions. Anyone can put frozen soup on and make themselves a meal.

Ben:
I find the microwave a boon – it speeds things up considerably.

Eddie:
I would be prepared to pay for a housekeeper to prepare the evening meal rather than to cook it myself. Preferably it would be someone living close by.

Allan:
I like friends around so I plan a large group to reduce the workload of individual visits. In fact its more fun. I organize only 1 choice of food and its a help yourself situation. Something like spaghetti bolognaise and salad is my ideal.

Sue:
Concentrate on barbeques where the men help out and it doesn't wreck the house. After all, I like to have fun as well.

Ellen:
Seeing I'm such a hopeless cook my friends seem to actually expect to have tinned soup and barbequed chook. Maybe, one day I'll give them a shock and produce something that I have made all by myself.

Marie:
I've decided to send the kids to cooking lessons. One is quite keen but the other is not so sure. I want them to learn the right way of doing

things. In the meantime, I'll let them have as much practice in my kitchen as they want and stay out of sight to give them a fair chance.

Steven:
Cooking is O.K. but the hate is shopping for groceries. I write a list out for the grocer and he delivers it. I pay for it and put it away and that's bad enough. I've worked out a list which has been photocopied and each week simply tick what I want.
Its more expensive this way but worth every cent.

Any Other Simple & Easy Recipe